C000230716

THE 1

John McGahern was born in 1934 and brought up in Roscommon and different parts of Leitrim, where he now lives. He has written three collections of stories, *Nightlines*, *Getting Through*, and *High Ground*; five novels, *The Barracks*, *The Dark*, *The Leavetaking*, *The Pornographer* and *Amongst Women*; and a number of plays for radio and TV, which include *The Rockingham Shoot* (BBC) and the screenplay for the forthcoming production of *The Pornographer*. Among his awards are the AE Memorial Award, The Society of Authors' Travelling Fellowship and the American Irish Literature Award. *Amongst Women* was shortlisted for the Booker Prize 1990 and won the *Irish Times*–Aer Lingus Literature Award. He became a Chevalier de l'Ordre des Arts et des Lettres in 1988, and received an Hon. D. Litt. from Trinity College in 1991. His work has been translated into several languages. *The Power of Darkness* is his first stage play.

by the same author

THE BARRACKS
THE DARK
NIGHTLINES
THE LEAVETAKING
GETTING THROUGH
THE PORNOGRAPHER
HIGH GROUND
AMONGST WOMEN

THE POWER
OF DARKNESS
John McGahern

faber and faber

LONDON · BOSTON

First published in 1991
by Faber and Faber Limited
3 Queen Square London WC1N 3AU

Photoset by Parker Typesetting Service, Leicester

Printed and bound by Antony Rowe Ltd, Eastbourne

A CIP record for this book
is available from the British Library

ISBN 0-571-16709-8

CONTENTS

INTRODUCTION

Many years ago I was commissioned by the BBC to adapt Tolstoy's melodrama into Irish speech for radio. Most of Tolstoy's fiction was by then part of my mind, but I was unaware that he had written for the theatre. In fact, I had somehow assumed that he looked on the theatre as frivolous. The people who offered me the commission felt that the play could translate naturally into Irish country speech because of the strong religious presence there and the absence of a class system; in a similar British idiom they felt it could sound merely quaint or antiquated and even ridiculous.

The play was produced and it was well received. One of the good things about a publication or a production is that it generally kills off any emotion that still clings to the work, and frees the writer. That did not happen with *The Power of Darkness*. Over the years I kept returning to the play. I began an original play, but elements from the Tolstoy kept straying into the work, until it was abandoned. Even after that, between works of my own, I found myself returning again and again to *The Power of Darkness*.

I had come to realize that the language I used for the adaptation had been too colourful and idiomatic and that it skimmed over what was at the heart of the play. *The Power of Darkness* is a perfect description of that heart and is uncannily close to the moral climate in which I grew up. The old fear of famine was confused with terror of damnation. The confusion and guilt and plain ignorance that surrounded sex turned men and women into exploiters and adversaries.

Amid all this, the sad lusting after respectability, sugar-coated with sanctimoniousness and held together by a thin binding of religious doctrine and ceremony, combined to form a very dark and explosive force that, generally, went inwards and hid. For anybody who might imagine this to be a description of a remote and dark age, I refer them to the findings of the Kerry Babies Tribunal in 1985. It is in the nature of things that such a climate also creates the dramatic hope, or even necessity, of redemption.

Several years afterwards, the play having gone through many versions, I showed it to others. What was pointed out to me, together with the many dramatic crudities, was that the play had moved so far from the original in the various reworkings that it was better to abandon the Tolstoy frame altogether and approach it as new work. After I finished the novel *Amongst Women* I returned to it for what I hoped would be a last time, as if it was new work, which it was, and was not.

I want to thank the playwright Thomas Kilroy for selfless and painstaking advice on the original version. In revising and reworking the present script I was given invaluable help and direction by Pam Brighton and Christopher FitzSimon, and by both Fintan O'Toole and Garry Hynes.

John McGahern, Co. Leitrim, August 1991

CHARACTERS

PETER KING, a rich farmer and horsedealer
EILEEN, his second wife
MAGGIE, his twenty-year-old daughter by his first wife
PAUL, their young workman
OLIVER ⎫
BABY ⎬ Paul's parents, poor smallholders
PADDY, old soldier, casual labourer

Plot: When the play begins, Peter King, a landowner, is dying. His considerable wealth was earned by his hardness and shrewdness in breeding and trading horses, but he lives in much the same way as the poor farmers he comes from. He has a twenty-year-old daughter, Maggie, from his first marriage, and his second wife, Eileen, is half his age. He expects them to work like servants, and he does not allow his money to spread ease or comfort.

His illness forces him to take on a young workman, Paul, the son of poor farmers who owe him money. Paul has a history of living at home, doing casual labour and womanizing. He is a potent mixture of good looks, sexual egotism, weakness and vanity. His mother Baby says that women seem to go for him like bees to honey. She is perfectly in tune with her circumstances. Her decent husband Oliver, Paul's father, is deeply religious, but he appears as slow-witted and ineffective as she is oily and worldly-wise. An old soldier, Paddy, who is fighting a losing battle with the drink, is lured into the drama, and gradually he becomes its moral voice.

The Power of Darkness was first performed at the Abbey Theatre, Dublin, on 16 October 1991. The cast was as follows:

PAUL	Sean McGinley
EILEEN	Bernadette Shortt
PETER	Mick Lally
MAGGIE	Aishling O'Sullivan
OLIVER	Tony Rohr
BABY	Marie Mullen
PADDY	Alan Devlin
Director	Garry Hynes
Designer	Frank Conway
Costume Design	Consolata Boyle
Assistant Director	Mairead McGrath
Stage Director	Finola Eustace
Stage Manager	Ruth Culleton

ACT ONE

A very large kitchen/living-room at the back of the house. The window and door to the right of the stage looks on to a large yard and a row of stables and old granaries and outhouses. The front door and the front of the house are never used except on rare formal occasions. At the back of the stage is a long stairs. MAGGIE *is reading a book beside the Aga. She closes the book and hides it beneath the chair cushion as soon as* PETER *appears on the stairs.*

PETER: Is there anybody there? Is there anybody there at all? Are yous all deaf?

MAGGIE: (*Standing up*) I'm here, Daddy.

PETER: Can you not hear?

(*Noise of agitated horses.*)

Can nobody hear? The young stallion must be loose. And if he breaks into the mares . . . Where's Paul? Where's that stepmother of yours? Is there nobody to do anything? If I wasn't so sick I'd soon put wheels under this whole house.

MAGGIE: I don't know where Eileen is but Paul's out on the road.

PETER: God, O God! It's enough to drive a man insane. What's he doing out on the road?

MAGGIE: He's talking to people.

PETER: Talking to people! He'd need someone on his tail night, noon and morning. Who's he talking to?

MAGGIE: They came in a Morris Minor.

PETER: They came in a Morris Minor! O God, O God, O God! Will you run quick and get him to see to the horses before the stallion breaks the place down. Quick! Listen to the racket, and they can't even hear.

(PETER *comes down the stairs as* MAGGIE *exits. He moves slowly to the window.*)

God, O God. O God, give me patience. They can't even hear when the stallion is kicking the walls down. This whole place will soon be in wrack and ruin.

(EILEEN *enters.*)

Didn't you hear the racket? There's the stallion or one of the horses gone wild. Do you pay no heed to anything any more?

EILEEN: How could I hear?

PETER: There are none more deaf . . .

EILEEN: You can lay off that now. I was out counting the sheep. You were crabbing about the sheep yesterday. The horses today. The cattle no doubt tomorrow. I haven't four hands, or eyes in the back of my head.

PETER: Paul should have heard the horses. We'll have to get rid of that Paul.

EILEEN: How will you get back that loan you gave them to buy the tractor when he wanted to go to England if you get rid of him?

PETER: His father will pay it back. Oliver is honest.

EILEEN: (*Fiercely*) Where, then, will you get another workman?

PETER: We'd be better off on our own. God, O God, did you ever see the like. Out on the road, talking to people, and the horses going wild.

EILEEN: There's work for two men here. If you let Paul go you'll get nobody. And I'm not going to do your draggin' for you round the winter with you up in bed dishing out the orders like Lord Muc.

PETER: We'd get plenty to work.

EILEEN: Why did you go to such lengths to keep him when he was going to England?

PETER: God forgive me, but it was the last thing I wanted. Who wanted him kept but yourself? There's the good truth.

EILEEN: (*In a rage*) I wasn't going to drag for you then and I'm not going to drag for you now. I'm not going to be dog and saddlehorse like your first poor wife.

PETER: (*Shocked, blesses himself*) May God give her rest. May God forgive you.

MAGGIE: (*Enters*) Paul has the stallion tied up.

PETER: What's he up to now?

MAGGIE: He's gone back to his mother and father. It was them he was talking to out on the road. They came in the Morris Minor. (*Looks knowingly at* EILEEN.) He says they want him to go home and get married.

2

PETER: Can anything be believed in this place any more? I better go and see what's happening for myself, though I'm not able to walk. (*Exits.*)

EILEEN: (*Recovering from the shock but even more enraged. Shouting after* PETER) Get rid of him, then, when he's away already. Well, I'm not going to drag for you. Get that into your skull, my lord. I'm not going to drag and listen to you crab any more.

MAGGIE: What are you shouting at Daddy for?

EILEEN: Shut your stupid gob.

MAGGIE: I know why you're shouting at Daddy. You'd never shout at Paul.

EILEEN: What are you saying? I'll soon teach your mouth manners.

MAGGIE: (*Running out*) It's Paul you want to be married to. That's why you're shouting at Daddy.

(EILEEN *lunges towards her but she has slipped away.* EILEEN *stands in a state of extreme agitation. She is still standing there when* PAUL *enters. She doesn't notice him at first.*)

PAUL: Eileen. (*Moves towards her.*) My father has come with my mother. The old fella says I have to go home and get married.

EILEEN: Why aren't you away, then?

PAUL: So that's the way it is now? You want to be rid of me?

EILEEN: I'm not going anywhere. It's you that's clearing out. That's all. Just here, to be lifted up or put down as you see fit.

PAUL: Easy now, Eileen. That's not fair. You know that I love you. I gave you my word. That can never change. Even if he forces me to marry we can still be together. I'd only be marrying for the old performance.

EILEEN: Do you realize who you are talking to? Do you think for a minute that I'd want your wife's leavings?

PAUL: How can I go against them? How can I go against my father?

EILEEN: That's right. Throw it all over on your poor father. Who's behind it all but yourself and your old girlfriend. What did you tell her when she came looking for you like a tramp last week?

PAUL: (*Weakly*) I promised her nothing. I warned her never to show her face round the place again.

3

EILEEN: What brought your father here, then? Who brought him here but that girlfriend of yours and yourself? One thing I can tell you for certain is that your poor mother didn't bring him here.

PAUL: I swear that's not true. How could it be true? It couldn't be true.

EILEEN: You're a grown man now. You'll have to get that into your head at last. A horse can be brought to the water but he can't be made to drink.

PAUL: How can I go against my father?

EILEEN: Tell him you won't marry her and let that be the end of it.

PAUL: What if she says she's in the family way and that I'll have to marry her?

EILEEN: Was it you put her that way, then?

PAUL: There were others but now they are trying to peg it all over on me.

EILEEN: Did you tell her you'd marry her?

PAUL: (*Affronted*) Tell her I'd marry her? I did in my bollocks.

EILEEN: Then you've nothing to worry about.

PAUL: If she says to my father I promised to marry her?

EILEEN: Then she's telling it on her own.

PAUL: What if he believes her?

EILEEN: The more fool him. You're not in short pants.

PAUL: (*Watching* EILEEN *carefully and apprehensively*) I'd hate to go against my father. There was a fellow from Cloone who went against his father like that a few years back and he came to a terrible pass. I'd have no taste for that.

EILEEN: What happened?

PAUL: A tree he was cutting with his brother kicked. A branch broke his back.

EILEEN: Then stay away from trees.

PAUL: They say you never have a day's luck once you go against your father.

EILEEN: That's all auld raimeis.* I've made myself low as the dirt, and all for you, and don't you forget all we spoke of

* other nonsense.

4

together. I'm telling you, if you leave me now I'll not be answerable for what I'll do.

PAUL: If I'd wanted to leave I'd have gone that time to England. You know too well that I stayed because of you. You know nothing kept me but you.

EILEEN: Don't forget what I told you then, either. You can be everything here in this house before long. It'll not be long now till you're the master of everything here.

PAUL: No one wants to step into another's poor shoes. I'd never want to even think about that.

EILEEN: But you'll not forget everything we spoke of together, either?

PAUL: How could I forget you? I've never cared for anybody the way I care for you.

EILEEN: (*Embracing* PAUL *passionately*) Nor I, either. I care so much that sometimes I get afraid.

(*The door opens.* BABY *enters, blesses herself.* PAUL *and* EILEEN *draw apart.*)

BABY: What my eyes saw they didn't take in. What my ears heard they've already forgot. Well, I suppose people are only young once, but it might be as well to know, Sonny Boy, that your master is out there. He's out of his mind with looking for you.

PAUL: I came in for a halter.

BABY: I've noticed that those sort of halters . . . No. Baby notices nothing.

PAUL: Is it true that I have to get married, Mother?

BABY: What would you want to go and take on a wife for, when you can hardly look after yourself? The whole thing is a figment of your old fella's ranting and raving. Now, run off with your halter and leave this whole business to cooler councils.

PAUL: I can't understand what's going on.

BABY: Then don't try to understand.

PAUL: What am I to do, then?

BABY: Don't you hear Peter calling you? Go out to Peter.

(PAUL *exits, confused, closing the door behind him.*)

EILEEN: Can you tell me what's going on? Is he leaving or isn't he leaving?

BABY: Arrah, what would he be leaving for? Isn't he all right and more than all right where he is? Am I right or wrong?

EILEEN: I won't lie to you. I don't know how I'd be able to go on living here if Paul was to leave.

BABY: Poor Peter, it's plain to the world, is on his last legs. You're a young woman, the best part of your life still ahead of you. What's happening is only healthy, and wouldn't I be a strange sort of mother to stand in her son's light?

EILEEN: I don't care about anything as long as he doesn't have to leave.

BABY: Then you don't have to worry your head, love. That's just the raving of yon old amadhaun* of mine. Once an idea gets set in his head, nothing short of a crowbar is fit to dislodge it.

EILEEN: Who started it all, then?

BABY: Well, our lad is sort of harmless like his father, and he's good-looking. The women seem to go for him like the bees to the honey. Who am I telling? You know a bit about it yourself, love. Before he came here he was working in town as one of the week-on, week-off fellas. They used to go into the American Bar. There was this girl working in the bar they were said to have got out of some orphanage run by the nuns. You know the sort.

EILEEN: Was that Rosie?

BABY: Rosie. Whether anything happened or not I wouldn't know. But anyhow that old amadhaun of mine got wind of something about the town. It wouldn't surprise me if it was all put around by herself. Orphan or not, she wasn't the first to nail her man in that way and she'll not be the last.

EILEEN: She can't be let.

BABY: Well, anyhow, my old boy got all in a tatter. 'He must marry the girl. He'll have to do right before God.' I tried to get him to see there might be more than one side to the story, but you might as well be trying to humour a jackass. Well, if the front door doesn't open, always try the back door, because you have no use going against the men once they get an idea. You must know it well yourself. You have to pretend to see it their way. 'Well,' I said, 'if that's the way it

* fool.

6

is he'll have to marry her; but first we'll have to try to find
out *his* side of the business.' So, love, here we are.

EILEEN: What if he still orders Paul to marry her? Paul is still sort
of in awe of his father.

BABY: Order, is it? Why the man wouldn't know how to order his
breakfast. Baby only brought him here to get him turning in
circles. There'll be no marrying. You can take it from me.
Baby knows which side of her bread is buttered.

EILEEN: Last week the same Rosie came here looking for him.
You know, in some ways Paul is very soft.

BABY: Softness is one thing. Marrying is another. The girl hasn't
a thing to her name but the clothes she stands up in. Paul
may be a bit soft but no son of Baby's is all that far astray.

EILEEN: If Paul left I'd be finished. I couldn't live here without
him.

BABY: Who are you talking to? Isn't it only natural? There was
never much jizz left in poor Peter the best day ever he was.

EILEEN: The very sight of him makes me sick, and he's never
done complaining.

BABY: I know, love. They get that way. What I'm afraid of – and
there's talk – that he might hand everything here over to that
sister of his. We'd be all high and dry if he put her in charge.
I brought you these in case they might be needed. (*Looks
around and whispers*) This will put him so sound asleep that
the devil wouldn't wake him. And this – I don't like to say
what it does – can put an end to poor peoples' troubles before
they realize they have any. There is many a funeral that's
followed by a fine wedding. I brought them just in case they
are needed. The whole world can see the poor man is on his
way out, anyhow.

EILEEN: I'm not sure I'm taking in . . . I don't know.

BABY: I brought them just in case. You can never think too far
ahead in this world.

EILEEN: It frightens me . . .

BABY: Maybe if the man was blooming it'd be different. As it is,
he's betwixt and between, neither in this world or the next.
Sure, it's an everyday occurrence nowadays. Doctors give it
as a kindness every day of the week, though they can't say

7

that they do. They do it in these new hospices every day . . .

EILEEN: I couldn't do it. I'd never bring myself . . .

BABY: Just as you like, love. I'll take them back.

EILEEN: Is that all there is to it? It's just like giving medicine?

BABY: With a nice cup of tea, love.

EILEEN: I'm not sure what I'm doing. I shouldn't be even taking
them in my hands.

BABY: I promised the man some money that gave them me.

EILEEN: Take it.

(She hands over money and goes to hide the drugs in a box.)

BABY: Now, love, don't let them out of your sight.

EILEEN: Nobody will look in there, but later I'll put them in a
safer place.

BABY: That's the kind of talk I like to hear. But if by any
misfortune they saw the light, all you have to say is that
they're for dogs that go around killing sheep. Actually, they
work very well on dogs.

(The door opens.)

PETER: *(Off stage)* Come in and take the weight off your feet.

(He and OLIVER enter.)

Now, Oliver, there's no use beating round the bush. Tell me
straight out.

OLIVER: Well, you know, whatever is right – you know –
whatever is right. *(He takes his cap off to EILEEN. She shakes
his hand.)*

PETER: Sit down. We'll have to think this thing through. Do you
want him to be married?

BABY: I don't see what all this rush into marrying is about. If he
leaves here and gets married what'll he live on at our place?
As it is we haven't enough place for ourselves.

PETER: You have to decide that. You have to make up your own
minds.

BABY: What hurry is on him to marry? To listen to that man of
mine here you'd think the world was coming to an end if he
didn't marry.

PETER: He could do worse than to marry. Marriage often gives a
man a more serious outlook on life.

OLIVER: It could be managed, you know. I've got a job in town.

8

BABY: A plush job at that. In the bonemeal factory. You should get the whiff off him when he comes home. It'd make you throw up.

OLIVER: It *is* a bit of a noseful, I admit. But it pays off, you know. Paul could do the shuffling round the house and I'd be bringing something in from the factory.

PETER: You've decided that your son should stay at home. That seems fair enough to me. There's just the matter of the loan. I'd expect that to be paid back if he was to leave.

OLIVER: Of course, Peter King. It wouldn't be – you know – honest otherwise. All we'd ask is to be given some time.

PETER: That's easily arranged.

BABY: We're jumping too far ahead of ourselves. The marrying part hasn't been settled at all yet. If she was a girl of a family we knew, it'd be a different set-up. But how can we take her word for everything?

OLIVER: You're blackening her now. She did no wrong. It was our son who did the wrong.

PETER: What wrong did he do?

OLIVER: Well, you know, you know, did with her what shouldn't be done.

BABY: Will you whist for a minute, you auld amadhaun? It's little you know about women. She set her cap at him from the very beginning. Now she's saying that it was him led *her* up the garden path.

PETER: If that's true it does him no credit either.

BABY: But everything rests on her word up to now, a word nobody would take but that auld simpleton there. Doesn't the whole of the country except himself know that she was the next best thing to the town bicycle.

OLIVER: There you are – you know – twisting, twisting . . . wronging the girl.

BABY: (*Mimicking*) You know, you know, you know . . . You don't even know what part of Ireland you're in. Don't take our word for it, Peter King. Go and ask anybody from the town about the girls that work in the American Bar and you'll soon get an earful. It's that kind of bar. They pick them specially.

9

PETER: Well, if that's the kind she is, maybe you should be slow to rush into anything. Marriage is a serious matter. It's easier to get into than to get out of.

OLIVER: She's being blackened, I tell you. I know that she's decent, and I feel sorry for her.

BABY: Will you look at him? Isn't he an ornament? Sorry for a one that'd chase after anything that moved in britches and no care at all for his own son.

OLIVER: I know what I say is right.

BABY: That must be a great comfort to you, when the whole world can see that you're talking through your drainpipe.

OLIVER: You can twist things in peoples' eyes but you can't twist them in God's eyes.

BABY: You might as well be talking to a jennet.

OLIVER: She's a hardworking girl. She's young and – you know – she has her health. She keeps herself clean. We're not as young as we were once. You know, you know – we're getting on. We could do with a young pair of hands round the place. But the main thing is that the wrong done to the girl must be put right before God, all the more so because she has neither father nor mother nor brother to fall back on.

BABY: It's plain that she had no trouble in pulling the wool over *your* eyes, you auld gulpin.

OLIVER: Isn't she a human being the same as ourselves under the sky? Isn't she equal in God's eyes? There's no other way to look at it.

BABY: Away on his rocking-horse again.

PETER: Take it easy. Now, Oliver, some of these girls aren't everything they make out to be either. What we should do is send for your son and ask him – straight out – what happened. He won't swear lies in front of his father.

BABY: That's the first sensible words I heard today. We haven't work enough for Paul at home. Any time there's a rush we can get Paddy, the old British soldier, for a day or two. He'll work for the price of a few drinks.

OLIVER: Often, Peter King, we twist things to favour ourselves and refuse to take God into account. And what we think to be best for ourselves turns out to be the worst because we left God out.

PETER: Of course we must include God. It wouldn't be right if
religion was left out.

OLIVER: If we leave God out of it everything sooner or later takes
a turn for the worse no matter how well it seemed to favour
ourselves in the beginning. If we do it God's way it may
appear hard at the time but we're right in our minds – you
see – you see – that's the main thing. We're happy. We're
doing God's will. The lad should come home and marry the
girl. I'll keep the job in the factory. We'll manage with the
help of God. Other people do.

PETER: Go and get Paul. We'll put it to him straight.

(PAUL *enters*.)

PAUL: I was sent for?

PETER: Where have you left your manners? A cigarette in your
mouth when your father wants to speak to you!

OLIVER: It seems there's – you know – you know – a rumour
going round about you, Paul.

PAUL: What sort of rumour? The country is full of rumours.

OLIVER: About – you know – yourself and Rosie, the orphan girl.

PAUL: That's a good one.

OLIVER: Is it true or not true? You must tell the truth before God.
Have you been – you know – you know – yes, fooling with
her?

PAUL: I haven't a notion of what you're driving at.

OLIVER: Yes. Fooling with her, committing sin . . .

PAUL: We all had a bit of fun with the girls. There was never
anything serious.

PETER: Don't try to slither. Give your father a straight answer.

OLIVER: You can twist things before men but not before God.
She's an orphan. She has no one to stand up for her. There's
all the more need to be straight and decent.

PAUL: There's no slithering. I've told you nothing because there's
nothing to tell. (*Getting excited*,) Why didn't she say anything
about Billy Molloy? Why has everything to be pegged over
on me?

OLIVER: Think before it's too late. A lie can't be hid from God.

PAUL: There was nothing between us but a bit of fun. And may
God strike me dead if I lie. (*Silence. Then still more excitedly*,)

Why are you trying to peg over everything on me when all the
fellows had a bit of a fling?

BABY: Do you see now? He'd believe everybody before his own
son.

PETER: It's all settled, then?

OLIVER: Remember, if a man does wrong he may escape for a year
or ten years. But sooner or later it catches up with him. God
catches up with him. That poor girl – you know. What will she
do with her child, and her all alone in the world.

PAUL: That can't be thrown over on me.

BABY: Once your auld fella gets an idea into his head it can't be got
out. It's a waste of breath trying to say anything.

PETER: (*To* OLIVER) What do you say?

OLIVER: He must do as he thinks right, but I only wish, I only
wish . . .

BABY: You only wish. You only wish. Paul will stay where he is.
We haven't enough for ourselves at home.

PETER: There's just one last thing. He's no use to me over the
winter if he's not going to stay at least a year.

BABY: Of course he can stay for the year – and more than the year.
As we said, we can get Paddy who is beside us for a few days to
do the little that has to be done round our place when the rush
comes.

PETER: He's stopping for the year, then?

OLIVER: For the year, Peter King, but I don't know. I'm not easy.

BABY: It's all settled. Signed, sealed, and delivered from this very
day. I know he'll be treated decently.

PETER: If that is all settled I'll see you out as far as the road. Paul, I
want you to check those horses. If they were seen to properly
there'd be no panic like a few hours ago.
(*Everyone exits but* PAUL. MAGGIE *enters.*)

MAGGIE: (*Startled at finding* PAUL *alone.*) You might at least have lit
the lamp.

PAUL: I don't need any lamp to admire you, Maggie.

MAGGIE: Go off with yourself. I won't fall for that old guff. And
there's another poor woman looking for you. This place is
getting as bad as O'Connell Street with the amount of people
looking for you.

PAUL: Who is it?

MAGGIE: The same girl that was here looking for you last week.

PAUL: You're trying to make a fool out of me, Maggie.

MAGGIE: Go out and see for yourself, then.

PAUL: What does she want?

MAGGIE: She wouldn't tell. She asked me if it was true that you were leaving to be married. I told her I didn't know. You better go out to her. She said she'll not leave till she finds out.

PAUL: Did they see her on the way out to the car?

MAGGIE: No. I didn't see them go out. She's waiting for you down by the stable.

PAUL: Why should I go to her?

MAGGIE: She said she'll come in if you don't. (*Laughing, embarrassed.*) She was asking me if they were trying to make a match between Paul and Maggie. The poor thing didn't know I was Maggie. She is all upset.

PAUL: What would you say to that, Maggie?

MAGGIE: Say to what?

PAUL: Say to marrying me.

MAGGIE: I'd do no such thing.

PAUL: Why not?

MAGGIE: Because you'd not be let. (*Laughs.*)

PAUL: Who's to stop me?

MAGGIE: You'd not be let. Eileen wouldn't let you. Your eyes would be tore out of your head if you tried. You'd get what poor Daddy is getting now.

PAUL: I better go out to her, then. I'll soon give sweet Rosie the road. You'd think she'd have got the message by now.

MAGGIE: Be nice to her, Paul. She's in trouble.

PAUL: I'm going to tell her to clear out with her bag and baggage and never to darken this place again. A stop has to be put to this fooling.

MAGGIE: You're nothing but an animal, Paul.

PAUL: She has to be shown the door. I'll soon give her the message. Why has she to come and pick on me?

MAGGIE: Isn't she a girl the same as I'm a girl? That's what you'd do to me too if you got the chance. I shouldn't have

13

compared you to an animal. People like you are far worse than animals. (*Exits.*)

PAUL: Once a man gets mixed up with women he never knows whether he's coming or going. He'd be far better to go out into the fields and eat grass with the horses. I suppose I better go out and see that Rosie. God, when these women come abulling you'd think there wasn't a fence up anywhere in the country.

ACT TWO

The same scene, some months later. EILEEN *is cooking and washing. A loud knocking comes from upstairs. She looks towards the ceiling in exasperation.*

EILEEN: He never lets up. You'd need a whole army to dance attendance on the man. (*Demanding knocking continues.*) He'd want you to be ten places at once.
(MAGGIE *comes down the stairs with her coat on. She is dressed for going out.*)
Is that where you were all this time? Beautifying yourself in the mirror again? Where are you away to now?

MAGGIE: (*Resentfully*) I was with Daddy.

EILEEN: What does the man want? Can you not hear the knocking. Are you stone deaf?

MAGGIE: It must be you he wants. He told me to go to Aunt Martha's and not to waste a minute.

EILEEN: (*Frightened*) What does he want with Aunt Martha?

MAGGIE: He wants her to take charge here. (*Starts to sob.*) He says he's on the way out.

EILEEN: I'll see what he wants but you stay here and make sure those pots don't boil over.

MAGGIE: (*Aggressively*) He told me to go at once.

EILEEN: I'll not keep you long and you better be here when I come down, I'm warning you.
(EILEEN *goes upstairs. She is not long. Returns very slowly.*)
He's not well. I'm going myself to Aunt Martha's.

MAGGIE: He ordered me to go and not to let anyone else go.

EILEEN: I'm ordering you different. I'm going to Aunt Martha's and I want you to go and get Paul. Tell him to come in this minute.

MAGGIE: I don't know where Paul is and Daddy told me not to waste a second getting to Aunt Martha's.

EILEEN: (*Very slowly and fiercely*) Paul is out in the fields. He's working the tractor. You'll be able to find him by the noise of the tractor. Tell him I want him this minute.

(MAGGIE *makes as if to protest but in the face of* EILEEN's
fierceness gives way and goes reluctantly in search of PAUL.
EILEEN *has bought time by this stratagem but she is desperate
and at a loss for what to do next. Her relief is palpable when*
BABY *enters.*)

God must have sent you. You didn't come a minute too soon.

BABY: What's wrong, love? You don't look well at all.

EILEEN: I'm nearly demented.

BABY: Poor Peter is still holding on, I suppose.

EILEEN: Still holding out and I don't know which way to turn. I
can feel them beating all around. I'd be better off in
Portlaoise. He's just tried to send for Aunt Martha.

BABY: What could he want Martha for?

EILEEN: He feels he's going and I fear he wants to give her the
money . . . put the whole place under her command.

BABY: (*Quickly*) The money is still in the house, then?

EILEEN: Peter never trusted banks. He keeps it in the safe
upstairs. You'd need six men to move that safe.

BABY: Where is the key kept?

EILEEN: Round his neck, but you'd want the combination. The
key is no good without the combination.

BABY: What, love, is the combination? Forgive ignorance, love.

EILEEN: Numbers you need to open the lock with. They're kept
on a slip in his wallet.

BABY: I'm afraid combinations came after poor Baby's day, but
where is the wallet?

EILEEN: It's either on him or it's hid. I don't know what way to
turn.

BABY: Has Peter as much as they say? They say he's a
millionaire.

EILEEN: He made a lot of money with the horses. They say he
was the best judge of a horse for several counties around,
and he never spent. Only yesterday I heard him say he
didn't want the taxman peeping after him into the grave.

BABY: Listen, girl. I've come to the safe conclusion if you don't
shift yourself quick you'll wind up with nothing in the heel
of the hunt, after wasting the best years of your young life
on the man.

16

EILEEN: I don't know what way to turn. Paul is no use. He's frightened. You can't talk to him.

BABY: Never mind about Paul. If you let this chance slip you're done for. You'll have to smarten yourself if you don't want to be out on the road. Has he had the priest and all that?

EILEEN: The poor priest has a pass beaten to the place. He anointed him yesterday for the fourth time. You know how funny poor Father Young is. He said when he came down the stairs yesterday that Peter has enough oil on him now to float a battleship.

BABY: It's good the priest was here that many times. Everything should be seen to be done by the book.

EILEEN: We thought he was going yesterday. We even started the Rosary.

BABY: Where has Paul been during all this?

EILEEN: Paul is like a child. He's no use. He's out. On the tractor. I sent Maggie for him just before you came. She'll have her work cut out to get him to the house but it's better than her going for Martha. I'll get you a quick cup of tea before we have to think. You must be parched. It's a sight for sore eyes to have you at hand. I didn't know what way to turn when you came in the door.

BABY: I am parched. I'd love a hot cup of tea. (*Sitting down.*) Did you hear about the wedding we had back our way?

EILEEN: No, what wedding?

BABY: This will be music to your ears, anyhow. Old Ritchie Coyne married the Rosie that had Paul tormented. At least that's one bit of baggage out of our way. She was damaged goods of course, but it appears Ritchie doesn't mind that. Years back there was an old fellow like Ritchie living beside us, who married a girl with a limp. He said he didn't mind the limp, since he didn't marry her for jumping ditches.

EILEEN: He's old, isn't he? I suppose he has money.

BABY: It's a comfortable enough place, but there's four children there already and with his appearance who else would have him, place or no place?

EILEEN: It seems it turned out lucky for everybody, then.

BABY: And it shut up my old gander as well. He had my ears light about the poor girl that had neither father nor mother. You could never get it into his skull that it's the breed of them. Anyhow, that bit is all settled now. (*In a whisper.*) Have you tried him with any of the medicines I gave you?

EILEEN: I wasn't able. I gave him the white pills once and he was like a sheet afterwards.

BABY: They have no strength at all. How many did you give?

EILEEN: Two. In tea.

BABY: You might as well be giving him cod liver oil. Did he remark on the taste?

EILEEN: He said it had a bitter taste. I had to tell him how when you're sick everything tastes bitter. (*Hysterically.*) I don't know why you gave me those things at all. I've hardly slept since I got them.

BABY: Now don't go blaming anything over on Baby. You took them of your own free will. If anything were to go wrong Baby would never heard tell of them. But, not to change the subject, I heard people talking about you the other day. Pitied you. They were remarking too how your auld fella could go and leave you on the road after sucking your young life dry. I heard people say it would be hard to blame you no matter what you tried.

EILEEN: Sometimes I feel so surrounded that I could do away with myself. I feel things beating around the place.

BABY: Don't worry about it, love. But we haven't much time. We have to find the money. Then we'll give him what's good for him. The poor thing will be off like a bird.

EILEEN: I'm afraid. Isn't it better that he be let go natural?

BABY: (*Viciously*) What's natural? Is it natural that he's trying to put his sister in charge over his lawful wife?

EILEEN: I don't know what way to turn.

BABY: If you don't shift soon you'll find yourself out on the road and his sister will be cracking the whip.

EILEEN: I'd still have my rights as his wife.

BABY: If he gives her charge of the money you can whistle for your rights.

EILEEN: (*Panicking*) I better go for Martha before he starts shouting. She'd be here already if Maggie had gone.

BABY: Are you out of your mind? Here. Do what I tell you. Put on the kettle again here. We'll give him a good stiff drink. Then we'll have to get the key and the wallet.

EILEEN: Suppose anything would happen?

BABY: There's no time for supposing. Just do what I tell you. Put on that kettle.

EILEEN: (*In awe and fear*) I'll put on the kettle.

BABY: That's more like it. (*In a whisper.*) Don't say a word about this to Paul. He's useless like that. He'd get all in a tizzy. He's exact like his auld father in some things.

(EILEEN *stops in terror as* PETER *starts descending the stairs. Holding on to the wall, he gropes his way down.* BABY *retreats into the shadows of the room so that she can observe.* PETER *is too ill to notice her.*)

PETER: Did you not hear me calling? Is there no way to make you hear? I might as well be dead up there for all anybody cares.

EILEEN: Don't you know you're not fit to come down? Now we'll have to get you back up.

PETER: Did Maggie get back from Martha's yet?

EILEEN: She didn't go yet. I told her I'd go myself.

PETER: I warned her to go at once. Has nobody any heed any more? Where is she now?

EILEEN: I sent her out to get Paul. You're not fit to be here on your own and when she gets Paul I'm going for Aunt Martha myself. Maggie is too giddy to go all that way on her own.

PETER: She's not half as giddy as what's left round here nowadays. There's no heed passed on me daughter no more than a dog. I want my daughter to go. I want her to go this minute.

EILEEN: Of course I'm not trusted to go. I'm just the skivvy. (*During the argument* BABY *stands in the shadows, a silent and sinister figure, unnoticed by* PETER. PETER *slumps into a chair.*)

BABY: (*Whispering*) Take care would you let Maggie go! We (*Gesturing*) haven't a minute. See if that wallet is above in the room. If it's on him we don't have to worry.

PETER: Who's that I hear?

EILEEN: Paul's mother has just got here.

(*As* BABY *starts to engage* PETER, EILEEN *climbs the stairs*.)

BABY: I just came over to see Paul and to see how things are getting along. I'm sorry to hear you're not well.

PETER: Paul's mother. You're welcome. But I'm afraid Paul has got out of hand.

BABY: I'll give Paul a bit of my mind, then, to see he does everything you want. My husband asked to be remembered to you. You've been always good to us.

PETER: I'm afraid I'm finished.

BABY: There's no use talking like that. Worse than you have got better.

PETER: No. I can feel myself going.

BABY: Well, even if it's true, everything is well taken care of. You've had the priest. You're leaving a fine family behind. They'll be comfortable. Paul will help them to manage for a while.

PETER: I'm afraid there's no one to manage. They're all wild with foolishness. I know all about it. Everything I've worked for will soon be scattered. (*He sinks even lower in the chair*.)

BABY: You're still the master. Can't you leave clear orders behind you for them to keep to? Then they have to do right.

PETER: Has Maggie gone for Martha yet?

BABY: She'll go the minute she gets back.

PETER: Martha should have been here by now.

(EILEEN *comes down the stairs. She holds the wallet up.* BABY *can see it but* PETER *cannot.* BABY *makes no sign.* EILEEN *hides the wallet in her clothes*.)

BABY: You'll have a drink of something. It'll give you strength.

PETER: I'm not sure I'm able to take anything.

BABY: If you don't take something your poor strength will soon go. Anybody can take tea.

PETER: I'll try the tea, then. Has Martha come yet?

BABY: She'll be sent for in a minute. There was a man up our way who thought he was done for and he mended in a matter of days.

PETER: No. I'm going. I know it.

BABY: I'll get you a nice drink of hot tea with lemons and sugar. Are there any lemons?

EILEEN: I'll get them from the dresser.

(PAUL *doesn't see* PETER *when he enters.*)

PAUL: So you are here, Mother. Is everything all right at home?

BABY: Well enough, thank God. We've our health.

PAUL: How did you find the man here?

(BABY *puts her finger to her lips and points to* PETER. PAUL *goes pale.*)

EILEEN: Where's Maggie?

PAUL: She's gone for her Aunt Martha. She said her father told her to go.

(EILEEN *and* BABY *look at one another.*)

PETER: (*Finding the energy to be peremptory*) Is that you, Paul? I want you a minute.

(EILEEN *and* BABY *whisper together.*)

How is it you're in the house at this time of day?

PAUL: Eileen sent Maggie out for me.

EILEEN: I told you that already.

PETER: Isn't Maggie gone for Aunt Martha?

PAUL: She's gone now. After telling me I was wanted.

PETER: Who? Wanted?

EILEEN: I wanted him. I couldn't be here on my own with the state you're in.

PETER: It took her all that length to go? Nobody cares. The place is in wrack and ruin. You can trust nobody. What's going to happen to everything? God, O God, what's going to happen?

BABY: Seeing you're here, Paul, why don't you help Peter over here, where he'll be more comfortable.

(PAUL *helps* PETER *to his feet.*)

Lean on me here. I'll help you over to the table.

PETER: Help me, then. (*Calls*) Paul!

PAUL: What is it now? (*As if expecting another rebuke; but he is taken aback by the uncharacteristic tone.*)

PETER: I may never have a chance to speak to you again. I feel I'm going. I want to ask your forgiveness for any wrong I've ever done you. I've said many a hard word to you in my time. Forgive me.

PAUL: What's there to forgive? I'm in need of forgiveness myself.

BABY: Have you no heart, son?

PAUL: Of course I forgive, but there's nothing to forgive.

PETER: For the love of God, forgive me.

PAUL: (*Emotionally, sentimentally*) God will forgive you. You've never done me any wrong. It's me that should be asking your forgiveness.

(PETER *is set down by the table.* EILEEN *makes his drink. As soon as it is made,* BABY *holds up the tablets and then pushes them into* EILEEN'S *hand.* EILEEN *cowers away.*)

BABY: (*Hisses*) Put them in the drink. We've no time. Once Martha gets here we're done for.

(*Trembling and shaking,* EILEEN *drops in the tablets.* BABY *then takes a spoon and stirs the drink.* EILEEN *takes the drink to* PETER, *who is too ill to notice her extreme agitation. She stands in a horror of fascination, watching* PETER *drink.*)

PETER: It tastes sort of bitter.

EILEEN: That must be the lemon.

BABY: It needs more sugar. We must have forgot the sugar. (*She gets the sugar, puts it in the drink and stirs it vigorously.*) It'll taste better now. That'll make a new man of you.

PETER: (*Drinks and then his head slumps on to his breast*) For the love of God, forgive me.

BABY: (*At once feels his pulse*) The poor thing is gone. Isn't he far better off than the way he was. In the end the poor thing went away like a bird. (*She feels round his neck for the key.*) Get a scissors. It'll be easier to cut with a scissors.

(EILEEN *hands her the scissors and she cuts the string round* PETER'S *neck and holds it up.* PAUL *begins to cry.*)

PAUL: The poor man asked for my forgiveness when it is me that should be asking for his. He trusted me in his house. (*Staring in recrimination at* EILEEN.) He trusted me in his house and look how I paid him back.

BABY: Enough of that old stuff. We'll need your help.

EILEEN: I can't move, I'm that afraid.

BABY: If you don't move soon you'll have the whole of your life to think about moving.

EILEEN: What can we do?

BABY: Take the key. You have his wallet. Open the safe. Get the money. Give the money to Paul. Paul will hide the money.

EILEEN: I'm frightened.

BABY: You've no time to be afraid.

PAUL: I don't want any poor man's money.

BABY: Hurry. Both of you. He was going to put both of you out
on the road and you'll be still out on the road if you don't
hurry. I'll stay here in case Martha or Maggie comes back.
Hurry. We haven't a minute to lose.

*(They both yield to her and climb the stairs. BABY remains on
stage with PETER, watching the door like a hawk. Upstairs,
there is the noise of them trying to open the safe. They come down
the stairs. EILEEN is carrying a cloth bag.)*

You got it open?

EILEEN: I thought it would never open, and then it opened all of a
sudden.

BABY: You have all the money? (EILEEN *helplessly indicates the
bag.*) Did you lock the safe again?

EILEEN: No. We didn't think.

BABY: For the love of God, woman, will you go back and lock it
quick. Give Paul the money. Paul will stay here with the
money. (EILEEN *hands the money fearfully to* PAUL *and goes
back up the stairs.*) Well, Paul, we'll have to watch out for
your end of it now.

PAUL: How – my end of it?

BABY: The way you're to live.

PAUL: I got by up to now, didn't I?

BABY: Well, if you did, it was poorly. Now you've a chance to be
somebody in the world.

PAUL: I don't know what you're getting at.

BABY: Oh, looking to your future and hoping that when the good
times come you won't forget your old mother.

PAUL: What's that got to do with anything?

BABY: Don't think to pull the wool over your poor mother's eyes.
I see what's going on. First, you have to go and hide that
money so that nobody but yourself knows where it is hid.

PAUL: The money isn't mine. It's no business of mine.

BABY: Sometimes I think you're as dim as your auld father, but
don't breathe a word of this to a sinner.

PAUL: I don't know what's going on. You women have everything

23

through other. I don't know whether I'm coming or going.

BABY: There's nothing through other. Once you get your hands on the money you're the boss. Women, you know, are very changeable. Once you have the money the whip is in your hands. Do you get me now?

PAUL: You women would drive a man out of his mind with your scheming. The poor man is dead. I can't even ask his forgiveness now.

(*Pale and distraught*, EILEEN *comes down the stairs.*)

EILEEN: (*Wearily*) It's locked. (*She moves to give* BABY *the key.*) It's your key now.

BABY: Baby wouldn't want anything like that to be found on her.

EILEEN: I'm going like a leaf. I don't know what way to turn. I better go with Paul and put the money safe.

BABY: (*Seizing her by the arm*) Are you out of your mind? Don't you know you'll be missed? Maggie will be here any minute. (*To* PAUL.) Are you paralysed or what? Are you a man or a mouse?

PAUL: I'll hide it.

EILEEN: Where'll you hide it?

PAUL: (*Suddenly smiling*) What are you worried about, Eileen? Don't you think I don't know how to make it safe?

EILEEN: I'm shaking like a leaf.

PAUL: (*His old jaunty, seductive self*) There's no call to be afraid. I'll hide it where an army wouldn't find it. (*Exits.*)

EILEEN: (*Left alone with* BABY, *turns towards* PETER) He's gone. There's not a breath. What'll I do now? There's not a stir.

BABY: Take it easy, love. Wasn't it a release for the poor creature?

EILEEN: (*Shaking*) We'll have to get someone in to lay him out. What will they notice? I think we are all going to be lost.

BABY: No need to send for anybody. He's not heavy. He was as light as a wren when I felt him. Many's the poor body Baby has laid out. There should even be some warm water left in the kettle. No need to send outside for anybody. We'll keep it all well within the house.

(MAGGIE *enters. She doesn't notice anything at first.*)

MAGGIE: Aunt Martha was in town but I left word and she'll be over the minute she gets back.

BABY: It's too late now, love. Your poor father, God rest him, is
     gone.
MAGGIE: (*For a moment she is stone-silent, and then she rushes
     towards* PETER *in a frenzy of grief*) What have they done to
     you, Father? Father, what have you done to yourself?

ACT THREE

The same room. Winter. Heavy rain outside. Nine months have passed since Act Two. Pots are cooking on the stove. EILEEN *is sewing. The door opens.* PADDY *enters.*

PADDY: Paul hasn't come home yet?

EILEEN: I don't know what's keeping him. His father is expected this evening. It'd be a nice pass if he isn't here when his father arrives, but even that would appear to be no bother to him nowadays.

PADDY: (*Laughing*) No bother in the world. Paul is letting the washers fly. He's living royal.

EILEEN: (*Sharply*) Have you all done outside?

PADDY: Everything is done and not done by half either. The horses are all watered and fed. So is the cattle.

EILEEN: Paul should be doing that work. Peter had no need of a man till he got old.

PADDY: Why did you marry Paul? That's when you made your big mistake. If you hadn't to marry him he'd have had to work. Never throw a dog a bone. (*Laughs.*) Hold bone in mouth and dog will follow.

EILEEN: (*Looks directly up*) I'm afraid I'm beginning to think it was a mistake, Paddy. Yet I loved him. I'm afraid I love him still.

PADDY: Love! Love, is it? Love flies out the window. Marriage should be the eye-opener. I came home and found my old dosey in bed with two men and she was that drunk she didn't know which bed she was in.

EILEEN: It'd be easy if love went away. I'd almost put up with anything before I'd lose him now. And I know things can't go on much longer as they are.

PADDY: You know you can still call a halt. Paul knows nothing about horses, and the horsey crowd have him all blowed up. He thinks it's great to be the master of a place that has the name of horses. They'll fleece him. Peter, God rest him,

27

knew his horses and he was hard. He needed to be hard. Those horsey crowd would take the eyes out of your head and tell you you could see better without them. (*Laughs*.) Was it a fortnight ago that Paul came home in that houndstooth jacket? (*Laughs*.) You should definitely call a halt before it is all too late.

EILEEN: There's many a thing I feel like doing. But then when I turn I find I can do nothing. You don't know what I've been through.

PADDY: It's you that has the dry hay – the washers. You can always call a halt if you have the washers. Just stop the washers. People can't go far without the washers. (EILEEN *looks up as if about to speak, but decides to say nothing*.) What brought Paul to town this time?

EILEEN: He said he had to get money out of the bank for his father; but if it wasn't that excuse it'd be some other. Nowadays he seems to live in the town.

PADDY: Did Maggie go with him?

EILEEN: Does he go anywhere alone? Doesn't he always take her to the town? (*Partly to herself*.) You'd think I didn't exist, the way he goes on.

PADDY: I heard them say something about a white dress. Is she going to be married? That'd be one thing less on your mind.

EILEEN: (*With feeling*) I wish she was. If she's not married soon it will be too late.

PADDY: Wasn't there a marriage arranged?

EILEEN: There was but it fell through. I fear they smelled a rat. People are no fools.

PADDY: Oh, there could be a rat in that stack, all right. That's the kind of a rat that (*Mimics a baby's cry*) when it comes out of the stack, could be awkward.

EILEEN: She's saying now that her father wanted her to have the place and be married to Paul. She acts as if she owns the place. And if I as much as open my mouth they're both down my throat. They think the whole ground is under them.

PADDY: If I was you I'd call a halt. I'd call in the washers.

EILEEN: I can't even do that. All that's keeping me going is that there is a marriage nearly arranged with young Mikey Coyne.

28

His old uncle married Rosie. You know, the girl that worked in the bar that used to come here after Paul.

PADDY: I knew Rosie well. I was often in the American Bar, but I'm afraid there's not much I remember. (*Laughs.*) I used often have to inquire if I was in myself the day before. Most times they used tell me I *was*.

EILEEN: If we could get Maggie married, then things might get back to normal here. But neither of them seems to be in any rush. They haven't got enough of their cake yet.

PADDY: I'm surprised you put up with it in the first place.

EILEEN: I had no idea. I loved Paul. I thought he cared for me as well. They fairly pulled the wool over my eyes. They only started to come right out in the open in the last few weeks. I can't stand it much longer. I can't sleep at night. There are times I can't stop my hands shaking. (*Listening.*) Shish, I hear somebody outside. That must be them back. Don't mention a word of what was said.

PADDY: I'll hop out into the hall till I see what the humour is. (*Exits.*)

EILEEN: On your life, don't go far. If he turns out to be drunk come back in at once.

(*A knock on the door.* OLIVER *enters.*)

OLIVER: God bless everybody here. Are you all well?

EILEEN: We were expecting you, but we thought you mightn't come because of the terrible night.

OLIVER: There's the car, you know; it's like an old tent. When you have a thing on your mind, you might as well – how is it put? – get it over with. That's it, get it over with. Do it there and then. So it's me that's here. Here I am. Is Paul at home?

EILEEN: He went to get money from the bank in town. He should be home any minute. We've been expecting him for the past hour. We thought it was Paul when we heard your knock.

OLIVER: Our old tedder would have done another year or, you know, two but nothing would do Paul but we get a new second-hand tedder. It'll be paid back, you know. We wouldn't want anything, you know, for nothing.

EILEEN: You needn't worry about that. I'm sure Paul will have it for you when he comes in. I'll leave it between the two of you. Now. You must be starving. You'll eat something. We were waiting for Paul. But you can eat something with Paddy. He's just gone out into the hall for something.

(PADDY *enters.* OLIVER *is very startled to see him.*)

PADDY: You're welcome here, Oliver.

OLIVER: Good Lord, Paddy. You're the last person, you know, I was expecting to find here. We were going to look to see if you'd give us a few days next week.

PADDY: I'm sort of surprised myself to be here, Oliver.

OLIVER: What, you know, are you doing here now?

PADDY: I'm working for your son. I'm more or less permanent here now.

OLIVER: You're working for Paul, *here*?

PADDY: I was working, as you know, in that last place but I fell by the wayside and they gave me the road. I ran into Paul after that and he took me.

OLIVER: Has Paul gone in for a new line of, you know, you know, business, that he has the need of a man?

EILEEN: (*Unable to contain herself*) He has plenty of business all right, spending as if money was to be found on the bushes. He's got so fond of work he'd lie down beside it. So he pays Paddy to do the work for him.

PADDY: Seeing that he has it, he might as well give it air. (*Laughing.*) Money doesn't exist if it doesn't go round.

OLIVER: That's not right. Too much money destroys everything in sight. It harms a man.

EILEEN: You have no idea to what lengths it has gone. Everything is being let fly round here. It's all one big spree.

OLIVER: Money is the ruination of the world.

PADDY: I know all about it. When I had money myself I was that polluted for weeks that I didn't know me own name. But now that the money is gone I've turned over a new leaf. The lack of funds is a great man for putting an end to the spree.

OLIVER: And where, might I ask, is your good woman?

PADDY: Good woman for sure, disappeared into nature. I have to admit I didn't search for her under too many bushes.

OLIVER: How can you both let that happen? You both, you know, are married.

PADDY: What else would you expect? An old soldier's wife for it! What do you expect from a mule but a kick.

OLIVER: It all sounds – how can I say – through other. It's not, you know, right. (*Silence.* EILEEN *sets the table.*) Had Paul something to sell in town?

EILEEN: No. He just has to get money out of the bank. But pull up to the table or your food will be cold.
(*They all sit down to supper.*)

OLIVER: I hope Paul wasn't going to the town to get money for me.

EILEEN: He's always in the town. The money was just an excuse to get to the town. (*Tidying up as the men continue their meal.*) If only his father would talk to him. He might get some sense. His father though is too good for this world. And the world thinks him a fool.

OLIVER: Did you say something?

EILEEN: No, nothing. Nothing at all. (*She starts to wash up as the men finish their meal.*) Did you hear anything about Rosie – the girl who used to work in the American Bar – since she got married?

OLIVER: Yes, now that you mention it. I heard the women say something.

EILEEN: Did they say how she's doing?

OLIVER: She's doing all right. She's a good girl. She works hard and the husband is a good steady old fellow.

EILEEN: Do you know anything about a nephew of her husband's – a Mikey Coyne? There may be a do between him and our Maggie.

OLIVER: I might have heard talk but I didn't heed it, you know.

EILEEN: We'd like to see Maggie settled. There's never enough room for two women in any one house. There might be more peace here if we were on our own.

OLIVER: It's good, you know, to be settled, but she's plenty of time. She'll be married long enough. She's young. She has plenty of time.

EILEEN: (*Barely able to contain herself*) She has a few days. That's the length I'd put on it.

PADDY: Pay them no attention.

EILEEN: You'd think he'd be here to meet his father. He didn't need the whole day in town.
(PAUL *enters. He is overdressed, in a pantomime of a horsey gentleman. In spite of his good looks the general effect is garish and ridiculous.*)

PAUL: Do you know who has come home? (EILEEN *looks up from clearing the table in silence.*) Have you forgotten me that quick? Do you know who has come home?

EILEEN: Will you quit your cod-acting.

PAUL: (*Very severely*) Who has come home?

EILEEN: Who else but yourself has come home? Will you come in and shut the door and don't be giving us our death. You're late enough as it is.

PAUL: You must say: the master has come home.

EILEEN: Are you imagining you're Master Wrynn now? A fine schoolteacher you'd make! An example to all and sundry. Don't you see who's here?

PAUL: (*Observing* OLIVER *for the first time*) I'm not ashamed of my father. I'm proud of my father. (*Bows*) How do you do, Father.

OLIVER: Drunk. It's a disgrace before God.

PAUL: Yes. I have to admit I had a glass or two. I met a friend, a most learned man.

EILEEN: Can't you go and lie down?

PAUL: Say: the master has come home.

EILEEN: Can't you go and lie down?

PAUL: First, I'm going to have a civilized cup of tea with my father. So put on the kettle. Where's Maggie? (MAGGIE *enters, fashionably dressed, carrying an armful of parcels.*) Come on over here to the light, Maggie, so that they can see you. Isn't she a knockout?

MAGGIE: Everything was scattered about the back of the car. I couldn't find the red thread.

PAUL: Oh, the thread is all right. Paddy will find it. I'd be most obliged to you, Paddy. As you can see, I'm a trifle un-capassitated. I got a few bags of nuts for the horses from the creamery. We are a bit short till the lorry comes round. When you take out the bags, Paddy, will you throw your eye around for the thread?

OLIVER: It's a disgrace. To put an old man out in the rain to lift hundredweights of nuts from the back of a car when you know you're far fitter to do it yourself. You're young, you know; poor Paddy is old.

PADDY: (*Rising*) That's form for the course round here. You sit back when you're young. You have to work till you drop when you're old. (*Exits.*)

PAUL: Don't worry your head about Paddy. He'd do anything for those horses. He even sleeps with them. He's fonder of those horses than of any Christian. Nonetheless he's a gentleman.

EILEEN: Do you want tea?

PAUL: Yes. I intend to partake of a civilized cup of tea with my father. (*He turns to* MAGGIE) Have you all the parcels?

MAGGIE: Except the thread – and this – this isn't mine. (*Throws a package on the table and then puts the other packages carefully to one side.*)

EILEEN: He's gone and bought her more finery.

PAUL: (*Trying to appear sober*) I've had a glass or two but I can hold it. That's the test of a man. You see, I remembered too about our old tedder at home. I got the money out of the bank to buy that new second-hand tedder that we saw in the *Observer* for my father.

OLIVER: You're drunk. You don't know what you're saying or what you're doing.

PAUL: I may appear somewhat intoxicated but I'm sober enough in my mind. I can settle the matter of the tedder right off.

OLIVER: This is a disgrace. A pure disgrace.

PAUL: Here's the money. I'm not a son that'd see his father short. Take it. There's lots more where that came from. (OLIVER *refuses to take the money.* PAUL *seizes* OLIVER'*s hand.*) Take it. You'll have to take it.

OLIVER: I can't take it. You don't know what you're doing.

PAUL: Take it. I'll not let you go till you take it. (*Tries to force the money into Oliver's pocket.*)

EILEEN: You better take the money. He'll give you no peace till you do take it.

OLIVER: (*Takes it, shaking his head*) This isn't right. No good can come of it. It can bring no luck.

PAUL: If you feel easier paying it back, then pay it back but I'll never ask you for the money. I'd never ask my father for money. Why don't you show us the presents, Maggie?

MAGGIE: What's the use? I've already put them away.

PAUL: Eileen here would love to see the new dress.

OLIVER: This is a foolishness beyond words, you know, and trumpery.

MAGGIE: (*Unpacks and displays the dress*) I don't see the use of showing them here. It's silk and you can see the Chinese print. A fat lot they'd know around here about China.

EILEEN: (*In a terrible rage*) Take your rubbish off my table or I'll soon clear the table.

PAUL: Don't be jealous, Eileen. (*Laughing. Hiccoughs.*) Play cool.

EILEEN: What are you ravelling about? (*Sweeps the dress off the table.*)

MAGGIE: (*Picking up the dress*) You can throw your own things around if you want but keep your paws off mine.

EILEEN: The table is for eating, not for showing off the belongings of a streepach.

PAUL: Take it easy, Eileen. I bought you a present as well. Play cool, ladies.

EILEEN: Whose money do you think is buying these presents?

MAGGIE: (*In a rage as well*) None of *your* money. That's for sure. You tried to get your hands on it but it didn't come off. I know all about it. (*Tries to push* EILEEN *out of her way.*)

EILEEN: Who do you think you're shoving? Keep your hands off me.

PAUL: (*Steps between them*) Take it easy. Easy on there. Play cool, lovely ladies, now.

MAGGIE: (*To* EILEEN) I'd keep my quiet about the money if I was you.

EILEEN: Quiet about what? Out with it.

MAGGIE: I know a thing or two, I'm telling you.

EILEEN: How would you know anything? Never gets up before the Angelus. Only able to chase after married men.

MAGGIE: It's better than poisoning them.

EILEEN: (*Stops in shock and then throws herself at* MAGGIE) What did you say? What is that you said?

PAUL: (*Holding her back*) Easy. Take it easy. Play cool!

EILEEN: You'll not make me afraid.

PAUL: (*Sobering*) You'll find yourself cooling outside the door if you're not careful.

EILEEN: I'd like to see you throw me out of my own house. I'd soon get the guards.

PAUL: Out you go, then. You were warned. (*Opens door.*)

EILEEN: I'll send for the guards. (*From without.*) I'll do some harm before I'm finished. This has gone on long enough. (*Door bangs.*)

OLIVER: This is terrible. Do you know that you've put your own wife out of the house? This is terrible before God.

PAUL: There's no need to look on it like that. You have to know how to handle these women. If you didn't take a stiff line they'd get up on a man. All she'll do is sit in the car or go down to Paddy in the stables. You don't have to put up an electric fence but you do have to know where to draw the line with these women. If you didn't know where to draw the line they'd get up on a man.

OLIVER: I've never seen such conduct. God, you know, couldn't be in a house like this. God couldn't be in this house.

MAGGIE: (*Folding her dress carefully*) Look what she's done to my dress. Wait till I get my hands on her dresses. I'll flitter them to ribbons.

PAUL: Didn't I put her out? Isn't that enough? What more do you want?

MAGGIE: If you'd left her in I could be tried for what I'd do. Look at my dress! It's ruined.

PAUL: Put it away.

MAGGIE: If you hadn't gone and married her that time everything would be all right. The place would be ours now. She'll do the same to you as she did to my father.

PAUL: There's no holding back these women once they start to turn wicked.

MAGGIE: It's strung up she should be. It's in jail she should be.

OLIVER: I can't stay on in a house like this. It's a disgrace. The devil is in this house.

PAUL: There's no use in this fighting. Why don't we have an old song instead? It's a pity there's no music. (*Starts to sing* 'Phil the Fluther's Ball'.) What we need is a shot of whiskey. Or a drop of that good poteen we got off the guards.

(*Door opens and* PADDY *enters*.)

PADDY: This house isn't half tame. They'll do for one another yet.

OLIVER: (*Rising*) Here's my place, Paddy. You'll need to warm yourself. I'm off.

PADDY: You'll do for one another yet.

PAUL: We might as well have a thimbleful of something better than the tea. Where's Eileen gone to?

PADDY: She's crying down in the stables. I'll go back in case anything happens. She's that out of her mind she could let loose the horses. (*Exits*.)

PAUL: Why doesn't she come in? There's no need to take these things too much to heart. (*Pours whiskey*.) What have you put on your coat for, Father. Pull over and have a cup of tea. What's got into everybody all of a sudden?

OLIVER: I can't. I'm going. Here's your money back.

PAUL: Where would you be off to? Pull over and have a cup of tea. Sleep the night here. The man that made time made plenty of time.

OLIVER: I can't. If I did it'd be like saying that the house was all right, when it's plain that it's well on the way to ruin.

PAUL: You're talking through your drainpipe, Father. How could it be on the road to ruin?

OLIVER: It all began when you swore you did Rosie no wrong.

PAUL: Are you still on about that ancient history?

OLIVER: A sin is always a sin until you go on your knees and beg forgiveness. You can hide sin from people but you can't hide it from God.

PAUL: Sit down and drink your tea, Father. (*Slurs*) Mother would soon bring you to your senses if she was here. Only for her you'd be in a friggin' monastery long ago.

OLIVER: I can't. I'm going. I'd be living with sin if I stayed.

PAUL: Are you scolding me now in my own house? I'm not a

child any more. I didn't ask you here. You came here on
your own bat. You wanted money for the tedder.

OLIVER: I'd beg on the roads before I'd take such money.
(*Placing it on the table.*)

PAUL: (*Holding him by the arm*) What are you getting all worked
up for, upsetting yourself and everybody else? The money is
yours. You need the money and there is lashings where that
comes from.

OLIVER: Let me go. It'd be a sin to take such money. I have to go.

PAUL: This is a nice state of affairs.

OLIVER: Come to your senses, Paul. Repent your sin. It's never
too late before God. (*Exits.*)

MAGGIE: (*Goes up to* PAUL, *embraces him, and playfully tries to take
the glass out of his hand*) I think I could do with a drop myself
after all that.

PAUL: (*Drawing violently away from her in self-absorption*) I'm
beginning to wish I was never born.

MAGGIE: I love you, Paul. You know I love you.

PAUL: Leave me alone. I wish I was bloody well never born. I
better get Eileen in out of the stables. (*To himself, as he
staggers to the door.*) Being in with these women when they get
riz is like being in with the devils in hell. They leave you with
no taste for anything. A man would be better to go out into
the fields and eat grass with the horses.

ACT FOUR

A storeroom off the stables and close to the house and backyard which are all lit up. From the house, sound of music and dancing and drunken shouting. PADDY *enters from the stables to the left of the stage, holding a rope and bridle. He stands listening to the drunkenness, torn between temptation to drink and disgust.*

PADDY: They're all crooked in there at the wedding, the women worse than the men. They said I could go in any time I wanted. They don't know me. Once I get the taste of drink at all I'm a goner. Then who'd see to the poor horses? (*Noises of people shouting and boasting.*) They must be starting to leave. Will you listen to the blowing? They are all big shots today. Big blows!
(PAUL *enters from the house.*)

PAUL: I can't stand it in there. (*Sees* PADDY.) Why don't you go in and have a good drink for yourself, Paddy? You've attended to the outside for long enough.

PADDY: I'm not drinking, Paul. I've learned me lesson. Once I ever get the taste there's no turning back.

PAUL: (*Goes to take the rope and bridle off* PADDY, *but* PADDY *resists*) I'll see to the horses, Paddy. You go in and enjoy yourself while it lasts.

PADDY: You'll not see to the horses, Paul. Your place is in the house. You're the *man* there. You don't need me to remind you. I'll see to the horses!

PAUL: (*Bitterly*) My place is more with the horses than anywhere in that house.

PADDY: (*Wrestling the rope free*) You see. The woman is out looking for you already.
(EILEEN *enters from the house.*)
You belong in the house, Paul. (*Breaks suddenly free and disappears towards the horses.*)

EILEEN: I was looking for you everywhere. Then I thought you must have gone to the yard. (*Goes towards him excitedly.*) I

39

feel it's you and me that are married. Our lives are just beginning. We can be ourselves at last. (*Tries to embrace him.*)

PAUL: (*Pushing her away, more in despair than horror*) I don't know what's going on. I can't stand it.

EILEEN: Everything is going wonderful. Several are saying it's been the best wedding for years. Once it is over we'll have a whole life to ourselves again. (*Tries to embrace him again.*) There were times this morning I thought we'd never get Maggie to the church but it is all tied, sealed and delivered by now.

(BABY *enters from the house, obviously in search of them, energetic and anxious.*)

BABY: Is this where you both are! Won't you have the rest of your lives for that carry-on? You'll be missed. Maggie is having these pains. I just managed to bundle her to her room. She's having a miscarriage, or what I hope is a miscarriage. We're finished if they start to smell a rat. I said she just had a small turn. But we haven't a minute to waste.

PAUL: (*Looking up for the first time at Maggie's name and then speaking slowly, uncomprehendingly*) Before she went to the church she had these pains. (*Breaking down.*) She said she was only getting married to please me. How did I ever get into such a business?

EILEEN: I knew it. I was afraid it'd happen this morning.

(PAUL *makes as if to go towards the stables.*)

BABY: Where are you making off to now?

PAUL: I was going to see if Paddy wanted a hand with the horses.

BABY: Paddy wants no hand. You stay here. You'll be needed.

PAUL: Needed for what?

BABY: You'll find out soon enough. You'll be needed all right.

PAUL: My head is going round in circles. You women are terrible.

BABY: Straighten yourself now. Stay here with your wife. Don't let him move a foot. The room is locked and it's away at the back but I don't want her shouting.

(BABY *exits with amazing quickness, rolling up her sleeves with*

the same sure gesture as used to prepare the laying out of PETER.
PAUL *and* EILEEN *are left facing one another as open
adversaries,* EILEEN *coldly enraged*.)

EILEEN: Don't stir a foot from here. You'll have work to do in a
    minute.

PAUL: (*Dismayed*) What work?

EILEEN: You and Maggie had your fun. Now you'll have to get
    rid of the fun.

PAUL: I don't know what you are hinting at. You women drive a
    man round in circles.

EILEEN: I'll soon tell you. Maggie had a miscarriage. (PAUL *starts
    to sob*.) You weren't so tender-hearted when you were
    battering me round the place, putting me out of my own
    home. We'll see what kind of man you are. We'll soon see
    what you're made of.

PAUL: (*In infantile fear and rage*) You want to get me into trouble.
    That's what you want.

EILEEN: No one wants to get you into trouble. You got yourself
    into trouble. Now you'll have to get yourself out. Do you
    hear them in the house? You'll be in some fix if *they* get to
    hear of your trouble. What will her husband do then?

PAUL: I'm going like a leaf. I don't know what on earth you
    women are up to. You have me going round in circles.

EILEEN: (*Quietly, fiercely*) Your mother will be here in a minute
    with your baggage. You'll do with it what you do with what
    the cat has. Or a dead lamb. You'll take it out into the fields
    with a spade or you'll throw it into one of the deep gripes.
    (PAUL *recoils in horror.* EILEEN *turns to* BABY, *who enters with
    a bundle of sheets.*)
    Is she all right?

BABY: She's a bit weak now but in a few hours she'll be as good as
    new. She's young and she's healthy.

EILEEN: How did you get to talk to her at all? She'd have tore the
    eyes out of my head.

BABY: Baby soon told her what is what. People have a habit of
    coming to their senses when they are told what is what. You
    go back into the house now.

EILEEN: What will I say to them in the house?

BABY: Tell them women's business and the excitement of the day, and it's probably nothing, but that the doctor said she had to be quiet till he sees her again. They're that drunk they'll believe anything.

EILEEN: I'll do that as long as this gentleman does his part. Take your bundle.

BABY: (*Thrusting it into his arms*) Get it out of sight quick.

PAUL: Is it alive?

BABY: How could it be alive the way it came into the world? Take it! We have to be quick. Every minute it's here we're in danger. Leave it in some gripe. The sheets can be burned after.

PAUL: What if we're found out?

BABY: How could you be found out? In your own house. On your own land. We have no time to waste on this talk.

PAUL: I'll not do it. Do it yourselves if you want. (*Makes a move to go to the stables but* EILEEN *seizes him.*)

EILEEN: You better take it. If you don't take it I'll spill the whole beans. Then we'll see how your tenderness will fare. I'll only keep quiet as long as you do your part.

PAUL: (*Taken aback by her fury*) What will you tell?

EILEEN: Everything. Who took the money and spent it? *You did.* I gave the poison and *you knew.* You're up to your neck. I'll not be long spilling the beans. Take your baggage!

BABY: Easy there, love. He's not that foolish. Take it, son. You have this poor wife of yours wild.

EILEEN: Take it or I'll bring everybody out this very minute. (*Makes as if to shout.*)

BABY: Are you out of your mind, woman? Here. He's taken it. Can't you see? (*Shakes* EILEEN *roughly.*)

PAUL: (*Taking the bundle, shrinking*) Curse the day I had the misfortune to ever get into this house. There's not an inch of me that feels clean. You can't make me do it if I don't want.

EILEEN: You'll do it. Or I'll not be long calling the whole house out. I've slept with Peter on my mind long enough. Now you'll have something to sleep with from this out. I have gone through so much already that I have nothing to lose. I slept with Peter on my mind through the night and got up to

42

see you and that hussy of yours make mud of me through the day.

BABY: Come on. We are on our own land. I'll go with you myself.

PAUL: I'll do it myself. But did you ever see such people?

BABY: He was too tender-hearted as a boy, love. It'll be all right. It's just hard for him. Go in and see that they don't start looking for Maggie. I'll go with him. (*To* EILEEN) Go in, love, before tongues start wagging. Once tongues start wagging they are that much harder to stop.
(EILEEN *exits*.)

PAUL: (*Holding the bundle out*) I don't know how I got into this. I wish I was never born.

BABY: (*Taking him firmly by the arm*) You had no say in it, Sonny. Neither had your old father. (*Just as she exits she turns to the audience*.) It's a good job old Baby is here. If Baby wasn't here things would be in a nice pass by now. (*Exits*.)
(*Into the empty stage* PADDY *enters, wildly drunk, carrying a bottle of whiskey and a rope ringed on his shoulder*.)

PADDY: Mad. All mad. All going to come down . . . a house of cards. (*Drinks*.) We came up out of the trenches. The bombs were dropping. (*Loses track*.) I can't (*Loses track of what he was about to say . . . Shouts*.) Whatever it was it was strenuous and continuous. (*Curls up in the corner and goes to sleep, snoring*.)

ACT FIVE

The curtain opens on the same scene. The noise of the wedding party can be clearly heard from the house, but it is winding down. BABY *enters, leading a distraught* PAUL.

PAUL: It might as well have been a child, and we threw it into the gripe.

BABY: It had months to go, son, and it is as well for us it had. These things happen. It's just like calves you find dead in the field. Often they're not half made.

PAUL: I wish I had been dead before I was born.

BABY: Take it easy, love. I know it was hard but with Maggie married and happy the good times will be here again. I hope you won't forget your poor old mother and all she's done for you when the time comes.

PAUL: How could there ever be good times again after what has gone on?

BABY: It may seem that way now but it'll change. What you need is a good stiff drink to steady your nerves. Then you'll be able to face into the crowd. They'll be away before long. Then you'll be sole lord and master round here.

PAUL: How can I face anybody ever again after what we've done? I can't face myself. The poor animals would never have done what we have done. The animals are decent.

BABY: Your poor nerves are playing you up, that is all. You were very excitable even as a boy. You don't have to face anybody. You can stay here in the hay until your poor nerves settle and I'll go and get you a good stiff something from the house. (*Exits.*)

PAUL: We threw it into a gripe. The sheets were soaked. (*Shivers and examines his hands.*) What did they do to Maggie? How can I face anything from this day out? What am I to do? What has been done to me? Once you get in with these women you can let go of your life. One evening I walked down the railway line with Rosie. I put my arm round her.

45

She came closer. I'm not made of stone. I'm only flesh and blood. I only came here to work, to earn enough to buy a few things for the home place, but I couldn't turn in the place but Eileen was there. I don't know why I ever touched her. Peter did me no harm. Then when he died I married her and that wiped the wrong out. I didn't know then that she gave him the poison. I was never able to touch her after she told me she gave him the poison. Then there was the wet day here in the stable that Maggie tried to pull the bridle out of my hands. We were cod-acting. Then the bridle ring broke and we fell in the hay. I wouldn't have done anything if she'd said even a word. She went all soft in my hands. Ever since then it is only in the wildness of drink I've been able to live. If I'd gone with my father that time and married Rosie we wouldn't have much but we'd be happy. There'd be none of this on our minds. We'd have our own lives. Rosie, oh Rosie, why didn't you keep me? It was my one chance. You should never have let me go. Why didn't I know it was my one chance?

BABY: (*Entering with a bottle*) A good slug of this will soon steady your nerves, but don't take too much. They'll be wanting you to make a speech before they leave. You can drink as much as you want once we have the house to ourselves again.

PAUL: I want nothing to drink.

BABY: A small slug will do you good, love.

PAUL: It will do no good. Nothing will do any good.

BABY: (*Taking the bottle to him as to a child*) A small sup will warm you, love, start you back to yourself. I know it has been hard for you, love. You were never able for much that was hard, even as a child. We could never even get you to pull the neck of a chicken.

PAUL: (*Drinks*) Why have you done this to me, Mother? I can feel it burn as it goes down but it still does no good. Nothing will ever do any good from this day out. Mother, why can't you heal your poor son?

BABY: Rest yourself, love. It'll take it a little while before you can feel it working. I have to go and get Maggie.

PAUL: (*Looking up suddenly*) Get Maggie for what?

46

BABY: Soon she'll have to leave with her husband. That's when you'll have to make your little speech.

PAUL: How will she be able to leave?

BABY: It's surprising what you can manage to do when you have to, when there's no other way out. She belongs to them now. She'll have to take up her bed and go with them.

PAUL: What if she's not able?

BABY: She'll be able. Women are able for a lot more than the men. They have to be. Don't stray too long here. They'll soon be looking for you to speak. (*Exits.*)

PAUL: Putting Maggie out too, stripping the clothes off her poor back, and she not able to walk. How did I get into the hands of such a pair of devils out of hell? (*Sees the rope, takes it in his hands and looks up at the rafters.*) There's only one way out now. That way I don't have to face anybody. (*Drops the rope as he hears approaching steps. BABY enters.*)

BABY: Get up, Paul. They're calling for you. Eileen had a terrible time getting Maggie down but now she's ready to leave. But she says she won't leave until she sees you. They're all calling for you as well. They want you to make a speech before they leave.

PAUL: What can I say to them?

BABY: You know the old stuff backwards. How happy everybody is at the sight of a young couple starting out in life. Two fine families united. You wish them wealth and health and happiness and may all their troubles be little ones. The usual old mullarky. Once you get started the only trouble you'll have is to know when to stop. They're that cross-eyed they'll clap like lunatics no matter what you say.

PAUL: I can't face them.

BABY: What's wrong with you?

PAUL: What did we throw into the gripe, Mother?

BABY: An accident. Nothing. Something that happens every day in hospitals, and out of them.

PAUL: It was like throwing a life into that gripe.

BABY: Enough of that auld stuff. That was your nerves. You'll have to pull yourself together. You've cut your stick so you better shape up. You'll have to put a face on it whether you

47

like it or not. Maggie had to do it and she had more to put up
with than you. Already they're beginning to talk. All you have
to do is to put a face on it. Otherwise they could start to smell a
rat.

PAUL: Who got me into this . . . hell?

BABY: Nobody got you into anything. I'll give you a hand up. You
don't even have to make a speech. All you have to say is that
like many a better man before you you've had a glass too many
but you want to drink a last glass to the happy couple and
that's the end of speeching. They'll clap and thank you all the
more for it being short. Come on, Paul. If you don't get up out
of that straw we're done for. Here's your wife even coming for
you.

(EILEEN *enters, dressed up, excited and tipsy.*)

EILEEN: It couldn't have gone off better, but they're all now calling
for Paul. Where has he got to? I thought I'd never get Maggie
down that stairs.

BABY: See for yourself, love, and if you can shift him you're a better
woman than his poor old mother.

EILEEN: Will you look at the cut of him? (*Laughs.*) But come on,
I'll give you a hand. They're calling for you. Everybody says
it's the best wedding in years.

PAUL: What's so good about that?

EILEEN: There was no expense spared. Everybody's happy. Come
on, I'll help you up. (*Takes his hand, but he pulls it away.*)
Maggie will soon be gone. We'll have a life together at last.

PAUL: (*Coldly*) Go back in. I'll come on my own.

EILEEN: It's no time for acting the fool in the straw. Everything is
respectable again. You managed to be a man in the end. I
never thought you'd have the gumption. All you have to do
now is go in. Then it'll be as if nothing ever happened. We'll
have our own lives for the first time. We'll be so happy now we
won't know one another.

PAUL: Go back to them, then. I want to put a few words of a speech
together in my mind. It'll not take a minute.

EILEEN: I better get back, then. Don't be too long, love.

PAUL: (*Gets up and brushes straw off himself*) I'll be there almost as
soon as yourself.

BABY: See how he answers to the young bird's call while the old bird is powerless. Always the mother has to give way to the wife. (BABY *and* EILEEN *turn to go.*) Will we wait for you?

PAUL: No. Go ahead. I won't be a minute. (*The women stop.*) I just want to think up a few words that'll send them away happy. It'll not take me a minute. (*The women exit. He seizes the rope.*) It'll be all over before they get back. I'll not have to face anything. (PAUL *starts to gather in the rope but finds it tightens. This puzzles him.*) It must have got tangled in something. (*He gives it a few quick jerks and then a very strong pull. This suddenly produces a roar from within the heap of straw.*)

PADDY: Hold on a minute there. You're not getting away with no rope. (*A very drunken* PADDY *staggers out of the straw with the end of the rope knotted round his waist.*)

PAUL: (*In amazement*) Why have you the rope tied to you like that?

PADDY: To keep fuckers like you from running off with it. I might be cabbage-looking but I'm not all that green.

PAUL: Don't you know me? Paul. (PADDY *staggers as he inspects* PAUL. *When he recognizes him he breaks out into hilarious laughter.*) What's wrong with you, Paddy?

PADDY: That's the best one yet. Trying to steal his own rope. (*Finding it all too comic.*) Or did they send you out to feed the horses? Is that all they think of you now? They'll soon have you made into another Paddy. They can take Paddy out of the bog. (*Finds this uproarious.*) But they can't take the bog out of Paddy.

PAUL: (*Anxiously*) Give me the rope. I'm in a hurry.

PADDY: I'm giving nobody the rope. I might be fluthered but the one thing I'm not giving up is the rope. (*Falls down.*) The drink got the better of me that time but the next time I'll do for it. (*From the straw.*) Maybe you're thinking of doing away with yourself? (*Finds this wildly funny.*)

PAUL: (*Petulantly, but anxiously*) What's so funny about that?

PADDY: (*Roaring with laughter*) You might be stupid, Paul, but you're not all that stupid. You think I'm fluthered, that I need a hand up out of the straw, but I need no hand. And you're not getting the rope. Paddy is no daw. Where the rope goes Paddy goes. Do you want to hear my history, Paul? I was a private – bad luck to it – in the British army, fought from India down into Burma. I was wounded three times, won the George Medal and drank it in the same year, and you ask who am I? You'd think I'd be a big shot because I came through all that war. But I'm nobody. It'll be the pauper's box for me when I go. I swore never to touch a drop again and will you look at me now? Do you think I'm afraid of you? There's not a man on earth that I'm afraid of. I'm sure only of one thing now: there's no turning back at this stage. I'll not stop now till I've the shirt drunk off my back. They gave me pack drill in the army because of the drink. Left, right, left, round and round the square, till the head started to reel, but that didn't stop me. I'm afraid of no man because I speak my mind. Who are you? they ask; I'm me, I tell them. Once you have to pretend to anything, you're frightened. And once you're frightened of any man, you're finished. I'm frightened of no man. We all came up out of the trench. The bombs were falling. The fucking Japs were everywhere. I had a machine gun (*Sprays the audience.*) And then . . . and then . . . I don't know what it was but whatever it was (*Shouts*) it was strenuous and continuous.

PAUL: Did you say there was never a reason to fear any man?

PADDY: What reason could there be to fear? Aren't they all made of the same dirt as ourselves? They all have to die. Look at them. One is bow-legged, another has a pot belly; someone else can run with a football half the length of a field. One is as grey as a badger, another has a shining head of hair – and how long will that last? – and what difference will it all make? They all have to shite. Doesn't it melt down to the same old shit in the finish? All the young women think the sun shines out of their arses and fellas like you, Paul, run around as if you had the meaning of life in your trousers. What does it add up to? It adds up to fuck all. What should you be afraid of them for? All they can make you do is die once, and then you're with the kings and county councillors. Tell the truth. Shame the devil. And tell them all to take running jumps. And whatever it was (*Pauses, forgetting what he was about to say*) it was always strenuous and continuous. (PADDY *passes out.* PAUL *seizes him by the rope and shakes him but it is no use. Noise increases from the house as if doors are being opened. Footsteps approach.* PAUL *turns to face them, like an animal at bay, but only* OLIVER *enters. The noise from the house grows louder.*)

OLIVER: I came, you know, to see where you are. The women say they can't get you to come in. They're calling for you to make a speech in there but, how can I put it, I think things are far from right in there. I fear God, you know, isn't in that house in there. And who is this, you know, with the rope? Is he dead?

PAUL: It's Paddy, Father. He's not dead. He's drunk but he makes more sense than most of the sobers.

OLIVER: Paddy is misfortunate, you know. He shouldn't drink but I never found any harm in poor Paddy.

PAUL: He said no man should be afraid of another man.

OLIVER: He's right, you know, in that. You should only be afraid of God. If you are not afraid before God you can't be afraid before man.

PAUL: If only I heeded you in the beginning I'd never have gone wrong, Father. It all began when I wouldn't marry Rosie. (*A clamour of 'Paul' rises from the house.*)

OLIVER: They're calling for you, Paul. You'll have to face them, you know.

PAUL: I can't face them. I've done too much wrong.

OLIVER: Then, you know, it's simple, what you have to do. You have to confess and God will forgive you. You don't have to fear anybody if you tell the truth before God.

PAUL: I'll confess to them before God and then I don't have to be afraid to face them as men.

OLIVER: (OLIVER'*s speech here is much the same as that of a gospel congregation*) Confess before God, son.

PAUL: I'll take off my shoes so that I'm barefoot before them. (*Takes off his shoes and faces the audience, with* OLIVER *proudly holding his arm.*) I've committed crimes – sins – and I want to confess. The first sin I committed was against Rose. I

51

promised to marry her, got her with child, and threw her over. Rosie, forgive me, for the love of God.

OLIVER: God will forgive.

PAUL: The next person I have to ask for forgiveness is Maggie. Her father died no natural death. He was poisoned. I took his money. Before that I took his wife. Then I ruined his daughter's young girlhood after it was left in my care. And then I threw her child in a gripe.

OLIVER: These are terrible sins, terrible before God, but God will forgive you.

PAUL: Forgive me, good people. Now I'll go and confess before God.

(Father and son exit towards the house. The tumult rises louder from the wedding party as PAUL's confession proceeds in the house. Cries of 'seize him, terrible, God will forgive,' amid general mayhem, wakes PADDY out of the straw.)

PADDY: What's going on here? Give me that rope. You're not getting away with my rope. *(Goes to pull the slack rope and falls back.)* Where are you, Paul? You're gone. Fuck them all and fuck you too, Paul. *(Listens.)* They're getting riz. What's going on? *(He rises.)* You're a poor fool, Paul. You'll never get that in your head. You're too stupid. You can only die the once. You'll have only the one small death and then your ... I must go and see why they're riz. *(Listens.)* It's strenuous and continuous in there all right. It's all coming down round their lugs, but not to worry. *(As he exits.)* You have the one small death and then you're with kings and county councillors.